Get to Know Foods from Other Countries

By Cameron Macintosh

I love trying new foods.

What do you know about foods from other places?

In this book, I will write all about foods from different countries.

Many people in India enjoy curry.

I like potato curry with spices and a small knob of ghee.
Ghee is a kind of butter.

I love to scoop up the tasty sauce with some bread.
I leave no crumbs!

Lots of people in the UK like gnawing on roast lamb for Sunday lunch.

They slice it with a kitchen knife and serve it with veggies.

Some people like to eat crumbed lamb cutlets.

The cutlets are coated in breadcrumbs and spices and then roasted.

They are so yummy with some gravy on top!

In Japan, people like to eat sushi with salmon and rice.

They dip it in soy sauce and maybe add a tiny bit of wasabi. But too much wasabi can burn a bit!

The salmon is sliced very thin with a sharp knife.
Then you make a wad of rice in your palm and add the fish on top.

This man has a knack for making sushi!

A gherkin is a pickle that is popular in the US.

Many people enjoy gherkins with sandwiches or wraps.

Some people don’t like gherkins, but I have no qualms about them! I love the tangy taste.

gherkin

In parts of Africa, people eat ghost peppers.

Ghost peppers are **very** spicy. They go well with pork and fish. But they can make your mouth go numb!

One day, I want to try one.

In Mexico, people make flat bread by hand.
They knead the mix with their knuckles and thumbs.
Then they pat it flat with their palms to remove the wrinkles.

Then they stuff the bread with all sorts of fillings – meat, salad and even beans.

You can put almost anything in flat bread.
You can't go wrong!

What other foods do you know from different countries?

You should write about them, too!

CHECKING FOR MEANING

1. In which country do people like to eat roast lamb? *(Literal)*
2. What do people use to knead flat bread? *(Literal)*
3. Japan is an island country. How do you think that affects the kind of food people eat there? *(Inferential)*
4. What do you think would be the best filling for flat bread? *(Evaluative)*

EXTENDING VOCABULARY

gnawing	Which letter is silent in the word *gnawing*? What are you doing if you are gnawing on something? What other words have a similar meaning to the word *gnawing*?
knack	How many letters are in the word *knack*? Which letter is silent? What does it mean if you have a knack for something?
qualms	What does it mean if you have no qualms about something? What is another word you know that has a similar meaning?

MOVING BEYOND THE TEXT

1. What is your favourite food? Do you know which part of the world it is from?
2. Which food in the text would you most like to try? Why?
3. If you were going to write about other foods from around the world, what foods would you choose?
4. What is something that you have a knack for?

TIME TO WRITE

Write about your favourite food and how you would convince a friend or family member to try it.